Errata
Jazz Piano Pieces To Grow On

Joni's Alibi, page 6, measure 4:

The Locked Store, page 32, measure 4:

Memories of Scotty, page 34, measure 2:

The Safflower, page 42, measure 4:

The Safflower, page 43, measures 10 and 11:

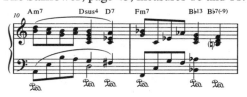

The Safflower, page 43, measure 20:

Jazz Etude No. 1, page 46, measure 23:

Jazz Etude No. 4, page 58, measure 36:

A Relative Match, page 64, measure 13:

A Relative Match, page 65, measure 27:

Summer's End, page 66, measure 5:

Party On The Beach, page 72, measure 2:

Party On The Beach, page 73, measure 14:

Shania, page 74, measures 2 and 3:

Ekay Music, Inc., 2 Depot Plaza, Bedford Hills, NY 10507
USA: musicbooksnow.com/steinway Europe: goodmusic.co.uk/steinway

THE STEINWAY LIBRARY OF PIANO MUSIC

JAZZ PIANO

PIECES TO GROW ON

Conceived and edited by
Edward Shanaphy

musicbooksnow.com/Steinway

The Steinway Library of Piano Music is published by
Ekay Music Inc., Bedford Hills, New York 10507

Editor-in-chief: Edward Shanaphy
Project Coordinator: Stuart Isacoff
Designed by Luke Daigle/Daigle Interactive LLC
Production by Anita J. Tumminelli

Distributed by Alfred Publications, Inc.
and Ekay Music Inc.

www.musicbooksnow.com/Steinway

CONTENTS

THE MUSIC

A NOTE ABOUT 'LAY-FLAT' BINDING

This special binding is designed to keep your music book open on the music stand. It will need a slight preparation on your part to help accomplish this. Place the book on a clean, flat surface and open it to a section near the front. With the heel of your hand, apply a gentle but firm pressure at various spots along the spine where the pages meet. Do not strike at the spine, and do not run your hand or thumb along the spine. This could cause the pages to wrinkle. Repeat this pressing process at various places throughout the book to break it in. When you have selected a piece to play, repeat the process again for that piece, and you may also, at this point, fold the book back on itself gently squeezing the binding.

PREFACE

This *Steinway Library of Piano Music* collection of jazz pieces has been created for teachers, students and pianists searching for music that explores various jazz piano styles, is enjoyable to play, and that can also serve as new and exciting recital and performance repertoire. The collection covers all of the various disciplines, harmonically and melodically, that go into jazz playing, thereby laying the groundwork for future improvisational explorations. The pieces range from 'easy' to 'intermediate' grade levels, and are so sequenced within the book. They have been meticulously edited and fingered for ease of learning and performance. Chord symbols have also been added to assist with harmonic analysis.

The jazz piano styles represented run the gamut from traditional jazz, stride, boogie woogie, ballads, the blues, bebop, to the modern idiom. Reading and performing jazz presents its own set of challenges: in the kind of rhythmic syncopations that only jazz requires, as well as in the tone production, touch, feel and spirit specific to the various jazz streams — challenges to which a student may not always be exposed with standard teaching repertoire.

All of the pieces contained herein are original compositions by some of the truly stellar performers, composers and educators in the jazz piano world today. Teaching in the jazz departments of such major educational institutions as the Eastman School of Music, New York University, and the University of Venezia, Italy, as well as in the private sector, the contributors to this edition understand the needs of piano students and teachers, and what it takes to make good progress in jazz and general piano performance.

We at Ekay Music Publishing are indeed grateful to those composer/pianists who have contributed their talent and creativity to this one-of-a-kind jazz piano collection, and to the people at Steinway & Sons for working closely with us to produce this and the many other piano books, folios and collections in the *Steinway Library of Piano Music*.

COMPOSER PROFILES

SARAH JANE CION

Sarah Jane Cion graduated from the New England Conservatory with honors and distinction in composition and performance. She was the First Place Winner of the 17th Annual Great American Jazz Piano Competition where the judges were Horace Silver, Kenny Barron, Ellis Marsalis, Benny Green and Bill Charlap. Sarah has performed with many veteran jazz legends such as Clark Terry, Etta Jones, Anita O'Day, Carmen Leggio and Bucky Pizzarelli as well as with younger musicians like Michael Brecker, Ralph Lalama and Antonio Hart. She was a featured guest on Marian McPartland's Nationally syndicated NPR radio show, "Piano Jazz" and her third CD, *Summer Night*, reached number 12 on the *Yellowdog* jazz charts. Sarah's *Modern Jazz Piano*, with a play-along CD, was recently published by Hal Leonard Corp., and her music is currently being featured on the WABC soap, *All My Children.*

BILL DOBBINS

Bill Dobbins is Professor of Jazz Studies and Contemporary Media at the Eastman School of Music in Rochester, New York, where he teaches courses in jazz composing and arranging, gives applied lessons to jazz writing majors and directs the Eastman Jazz Enseble and Eastman Studio Orchestra. As a pianist he has performed with classical orchestras and chamber ensembles under the direction of Pierre Boulez, Lukas Foss, and Louis Lane, as well as performing and recording with such jazz artists as Clark Terry, Al Cohn, Red Mitchell, Phil Woods, Bill Goodwin, Dave Liebman, John Marshall, and John Goldsby. He was a prizewinner in the 1972

International Gaudeamus Competition for interpreters of contemporary music, and has been the recipient of several jazz composition grants from the Ohio Arts Council and the National Endowment for the Arts.

In 1994, Bill was principal director of the WDR Big Band in Cologne, Germany, is now guest conductor of that ensemble, along with the Netherlands Metropole Orchestra in Hilversum.

DON FRIEDMAN

Veteran jazz pianist Don Friedman began his career in the mid-1950s in Los Angeles with ensembles that included such stellar jazz figures as Shorty Rogers, Chet Baker, Ornette Coleman and Scott LaFaro. Soon after, he joined Dexter Gordon's band. In 1956, Buddy DeFranco hired him for a tour that included New York's Birdland and Basin Street, and Don decided to move to the Big Apple, where he quickly became an in-demand pianist for artists like Pepper Adams, Jimmy Guiffre, Charles Lloyd, Elvin Jones and Herbie Mann. He signed on as a recording artist with Riverside records from 1961 through 1964, producing several records that earned top ratings in the magazine *Downbeat*. His fourth record included performances with guitarist Attila Zoller, with whom he had formed a close friendship. By 1965 Don was awarded the title "New Star" in *Downbeat*'s annual Critic's Poll. In the late 60s, he began an ongoing association with trumpet great Clark Terry which continues to this day. He currently enjoys a flourishing international career, and also teaches in the jazz department of New York University.

Since 2002, Don has recorded four trio albums (*Waltz for Debby, My Favorite Things,*

Timeless and *Scarborough Fair*), as well as a recent live performance at Germany's Jazz Baltica Festival. His regular trio in New York includes either Martin Wind or Ed Schueller on bass and Tony Jefferson on drums.

DICK HYMAN

Dick Hyman's extraordinary accomplishments as a pianist, organist, improviser, composer, arranger and conductor are legendary. Dick has more than 150 albums recorded under his own name, and his achievements have been well documented by the many awards, honors and citations he has received. These include his induction into the Jazz Hall of Fame, seven Most Valuable Player Awards from the National Academy of Recording Arts & Sciences, and Emmy Awards for his original musical score for *Sunshine's on the Way* and a PBS special on Eubie Blake.

Throughout his career Dick has performed with a veritable *Who's Who* of jazz greats, including Charlie Parker, Lester Young, Red Norvo, Benny Goodman, Ruby Braff, George Shearing, Derek Smith, Marian McPartland, Roger Kellaway, Ralph Sutton and Dick Wellstood. In the pop world, he has been heard on the recordings of Andre Kostelanetz, Percy Faith, Tony Bennett and Perry Como. He founded two long-running concert series in New York City, *Jazz in July* and *Jazz Piano at the Y*, and he is the jazz advisor of the Oregon Festival of American Music.

Also a highly respected composer and arranger, Dick has written scores for Count Basie, the Mills Brothers, the Boston Pops, Marilyn Horne, Doc Severinsen and others. He served as composer, arranger and/or conductor for Woody Allen's *Zelig, The Purple Rose of Cairo, Broadway Danny Rose, Stardust Memories, Hannah and Her Sisters, Radio Days, Bullets Over Broadway, Mighty Aphrodite, Everyone Says I Love You* and, most recently, *Sweet and Lowdown*. He has also lent his musical talents to the films *Moonstruck, Scott Joplin — King of Ragtime, The Lemon Sisters* and *Alan and Naomi*. His period arrangements were heard in *Billy Bathgate,* and as a studio pianist, he played on the soundtracks of *The Godfather, The Wiz* and *The Night They Raided Minsky's.* For the stage, Mr. Hyman orchestrated the hit Broadway musical *Sugar Babies.* Among the three pieces he contributed to this volume, Dick singles out *Stride Piano Playin' On Waikiki* as an unlikely amalgamation of two cultures, like Hoagy Carmichael's *Hong Kong Blues*.

STUART ISACOFF

Stuart Isacoff, a pianist, composer and writer, is founding Editor of the magazine *Piano Today* and Executive Editor of *Sheet Music Magazine*. He is a recipient of the ASCAP Deems Taylor Award for excellence in writing about music, and has contributed numerous articles to such publications as *The New York Times, The Wall Street Journal, The New York Sun, The Grove Dictionary of American Music, Musical America, Chamber Music, Symphony,* and others. In addition to numerous books of original compositions, arrangements and musical instruction published by Ekay Music, G. Schirmer, Associated Music Publishers, Boosey & Hawkes, Warner Bros., Carl Fischer and Music Sales Corp., he is the author of the critically acclaimed *Temperament: How Music Became a Battleground for the Great Minds of Western Civilization* (Alfred A. Knopf and Vintage in the United States). He has taught improvisation and arranging, as well as the theory, history and philosophy of music at

William Paterson University, Brooklyn College, and Purchase College of the State University of New York, and has given lecture-recitals and workshops at such prestigious venues as Lincoln Center in New York, the Verbier Festival and Academy in Switzerland, the Gilmore Keyboard Festival in Michigan, Sarah Lawrence College, the Gina Bachauer Foundation in Utah, and the Van Cliburn Piano Institute in Texas.

Stuart Isacoff was a private piano student of the late great jazz pianist, Sir Roland Hanna, who encouraged his desire to combine classical repertoire with improvisation. As a result, on the concert stage he often "marries" classical works with musically similar pieces from the jazz and pop repertoire, improvising on the combinations in order to bridge musical ideas written centuries and continents apart, and to dissolve what he considers the artificial walls between musical genres.

ANDY LAVERNE

Jazz pianist, composer, and arranger Andy LaVerne studied at Juilliard, Berklee, and the New England Conservatory, and took private lessons from legendary jazz pianist Bill Evans. The list of musicians with whom LaVerne has worked reads like a *Who's Who* in jazz: Frank Sinatra, Stan Getz, Woody Herman, Dizzy Gillespie, Chick Corea, Lionel Hampton, Michael Brecker, Elvin Jones, and numerous others. A prolific recording artist, his projects as a leader number over 50. Andy is also a prominent jazz educator, having released a series of instructional videos, *Guide to Modern Jazz Piano, Vols. 1 &, 2,* and *Jazz Piano Standards* (Homespun Tapes), featuring the Yamaha Disklavier. He also produced a video, *In Concert* (Homespun Tapes), with guitarist John Abercrombie. He is the author of *Handbook of Chord Substitutions* (Ekay Music) *Tons of Runs*

(Ekay Music), *Bill Evans Compositions: 19 Solo Piano Arrangements* (TRO) and is the pianist on *The Chick Corea Play-Along Collection* (Hal Leonard). *The Music Of Andy LaVerne* (SteepleChase Publications) has recently been published. Forthcoming are *Keyboard's Jazz Piano Compendium* (BackBeat Books), and *Jazz Bach, and Jazz Chopin* (Mel Bay). He has many play-along offerings with Aebersold Jazz.

Andy is a frequent contributor (since 1986) to both *Keyboard Magazine,* and the magazine *Piano Today.* His articles have also appeared in *Down Beat, Jazz Improv, Piano Quarterly, Jazz and Keyboard Workshop,* and *JazzOne.* He is the recipient of five Jazz Fellowships from the National Endowment for the Arts, and was a winner in the 2000 John Lennon Songwriting contest for his tune "Shania." He has appeared at concerts, festivals, and clubs throughout the world, and has also given clinics and master classes at universities, colleges, and conservatories worldwide. Recently he toured and recorded with legendary singer/songwriter Neil Sedaka. Andy LaVerne is Professor of Jazz Piano at The Hartt School (University of Hartford), and is also on the faculty of the Aebersold Summer Jazz Workshops.

NOREEN GREY LIENHARD

Noreen is a contributing editor and arranger for both *Piano Today* magazine and *Sheet Music Magazine.* Her piano books, and books for which she has contributed piano renditions, including *It's Easy To Be Great, Professional Stylings for the Solo Pianist,* and *Keyboard Runs for the Pop & Jazz Stylist* are among the most sought-after on the market today. A remarkable pianist, she has performed with such jazz luminaries as drummer Joe Morello, saxophonist Pepper Adams, trumpeters Howard McGhee and Clark Terry, and can be heard on bassist Rufus Reid's CD, *Back To Front.*

She has been featured on Marian McPartland's *Piano Jazz*, the National Public Radio show, and can be heard on the Christmas CD, *An NPR Jazz Christmas Vol. 2 – Marian McPartland and Friends*. Noreen's newest project for Ekay Music, a play-along collection of jazz improvisations on timeless standards, will soon be released.

RICCARDO SCIVALES

Riccardo Scivales was born in Venezia, Italy, where he currently resides. He is the author, most recently, of the Steinway Library of Piano Music book *Jazz Piano: The Left Hand*, as well as of the books *Harlem Stride Piano Solos, The Right Hand According To Tatum,* and *The Soul of Blues, Stride & Swing Piano* (all published by Ekay Music, Inc.), *Dick Wellstood: The Art Of Jazz And Blues Piano, Volume 1* (Soliloquy Music, London, UK), *Southern-Fried Blues, Echoes Of Venice, Dick Wellstood Jazz Piano Solos, Famous Italian Songs* and *Famous Italian Opera Arias* (Neil A. Kjos Music Company, San Diego, California). With Giannantonio Mutto, he co-authored the collections *Blues Piano* and *Jazz, Blues & Ragtime Piano* (Mela Music, Bussolengo, Italy). *Play Like A Pro, Keyboard Workshop, 500 Great Piano Intros* (Ekay Music, Inc.) and *Gershwin*, edited by G. Vinay (EDT, Torino, Italy).

He is a regular contributor and consulting editor to the magazine *Piano Today* and many of his essays, piano arrangements, compositions and transcriptions have also appeared in *The Piano Stylist, Keyboard Classics, Ring Shout, Musica Oggi, Il Sismografo, Musica Jazz, Rassegna Veneta di Studi Musicali, Il Giornale della Musica, Venezia Art, Jazz* and *Blu Jazz*—in Italy and the United States. Mr. Scivales teaches the history of jazz and Latin music at the University of Venezia and has written thousands of radio programs on jazz for

RAI-Radiotelevisione Italiana. He also gives lectures and master classes in conservatories and music schools, and is an active performer with his own *Mi Ritmo* Latin sextet. As arranged by tango pianist Giannantonio Mutto, many of Riccardo's Latin compositions are performed by the classical chamber ensembles Quartetto Note Insolite, Duo Giannantonio Mutto/Leonardo Sapere, and Quintetto Pianoforte e Archi.

ALAN SIMON

When Alan Simon toured with Lionel Hampton, his appearance at the jazz festival in Nice, France, prompted the following observation by a critic from the *Jazz Journal International*: "Hamp's pianist played lovely, swinging, and at times, quite majestic piano, and seemed quite undaunted by the varying stylistic requirements of Hamp's repertoire." A native New Yorker, Alan has shared the stage with such performers as Dizzy Gillespie, Anita O'Day, Toots Thielemans, Slam Stewart and Slide Hampton, to name but a few. He was described as "a wonderful and consummate piano man" by *The Chicago Observer* for his playing on *Rainsplash*, his CD on the Cadence label. He has toured extensively around the United States and abroad, both in concert and as music educator, and has appeared in jazz festivals in South America and in Europe.

A student of both classical and jazz piano, Alan graduated from the City University of New York with a Bachelor of Arts degree in music. He serves on the music faculty of the Westport School of Music and the Hotchkiss School, both located in Connecticut. Other Ekay Music publications Alan has contributed to include *500 Piano Intros for the Great Standards* and *Piano Stylings of Classic Christmas Carols*.

JOAN STILES

Joan Stiles is a pianist and arranger and a member of the jazz faculties of both The Manhattan School of Music and New School University in New York City. Joan's CD, *Love Call* (Zoho Music), which reached the top ten airplay list for jazz radio stations across the U.S., features an octet arrangement of her piece *Spherical*, included in this volume.

Joan Stiles began her musical education as a classical musician, earning a Masters Degree and completing coursework for a Doctorate in music theory before earning a second Masters Degree in jazz. Her solid training is evident in the skillful "reinterpretations" of the great American songbooks on *Love Call*. Ms. Stiles has been especially interested in the music of the late Mary Lou Williams, offering lectures on her life and works and performing an ongoing concert series, "Mostly Mary Lou," with such jazz artists as Warren Vache, Jerry Dodgion, Lewis Nash and Steve Wilson. At this writing, her second album, a sextet outing entitled *Hurley-Burley*, is about to be released.

Here is her description of the music included in this collection: "*Spherical* is my homage to Thelonious 'Sphere' Monk. After playing the 'head in' (bars 1-12), try improvising over the blues form and then play the 'head out' (bars 13-36). You can simplify the chord changes as follows: F7/Bb7/F7/F7/Bb7/Bb7/F7/F7/Gm7/C7/F7/C7. Enjoy creating your own thematic variations by emphasizing notes from the F blues scale—F, Ab, Bb, B, C, Eb, and F. To get comfortable with the '2 against 3' rhythmic conflict in bars 12-13, 23-24, etc., practice these figures hands separately at first. You might enjoy hearing the octet version of *Spherical* on my CD, *Love Call*, which features solos by Warren Vache and Frank Wess."

THE
MUSIC

CIRCLES
to Roland Hanna

Stuart Isacoff

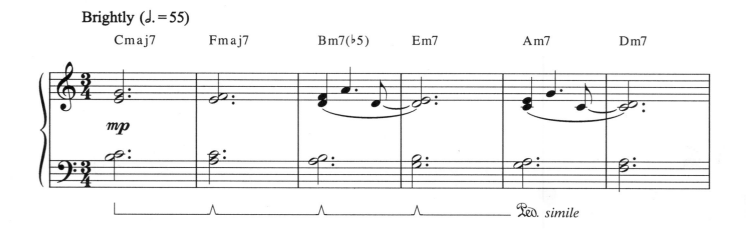

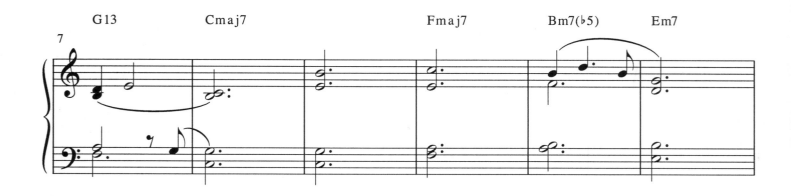

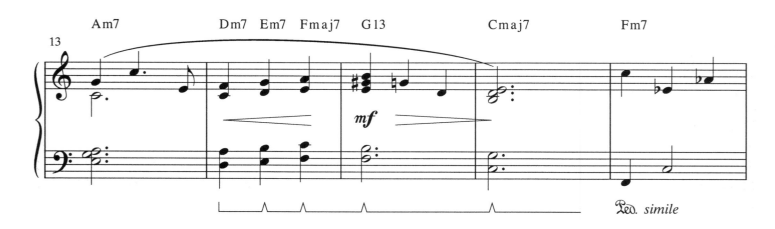

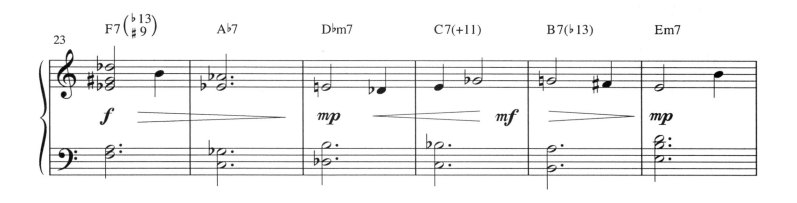

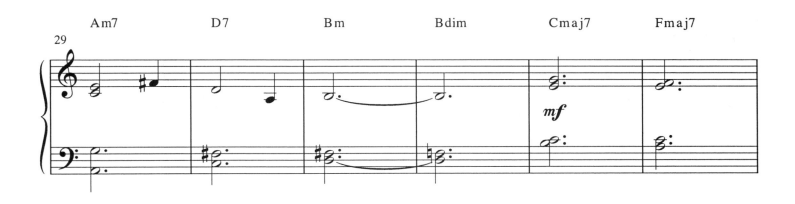

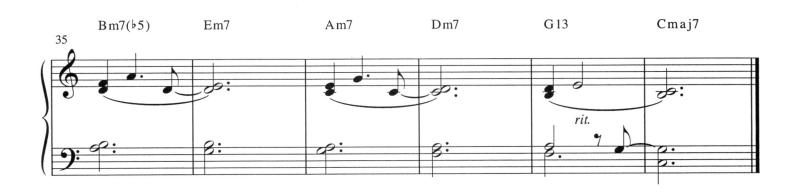

RESOLVE

Andy LaVerne

JONI'S ALIBI

Sarah Jane Cion

LOVELY DAY

Sarah Jane Cion

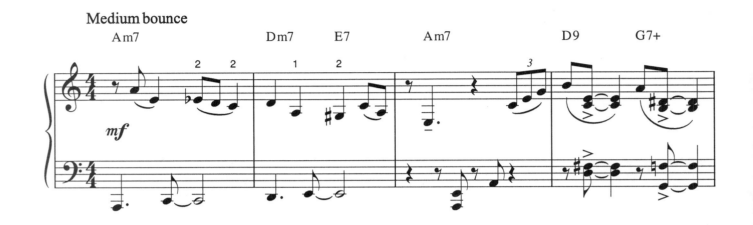

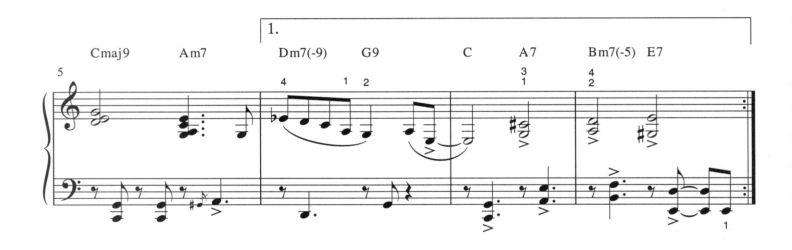

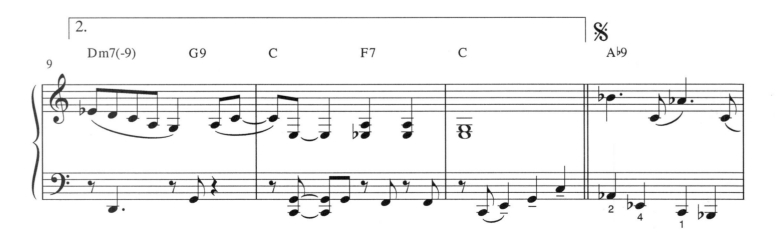

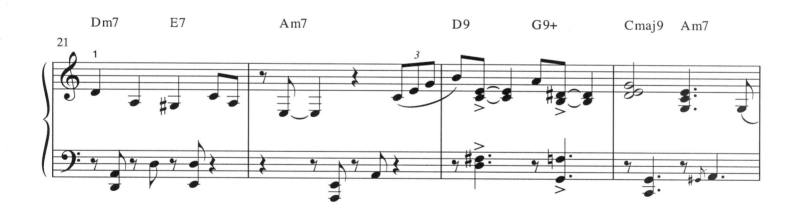

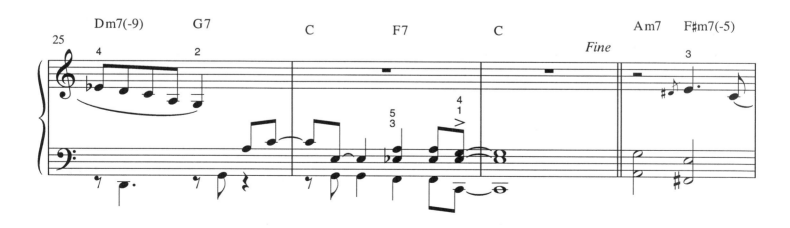

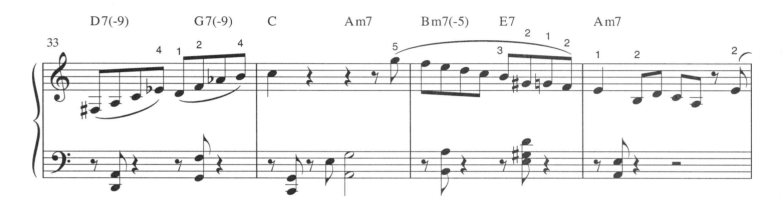

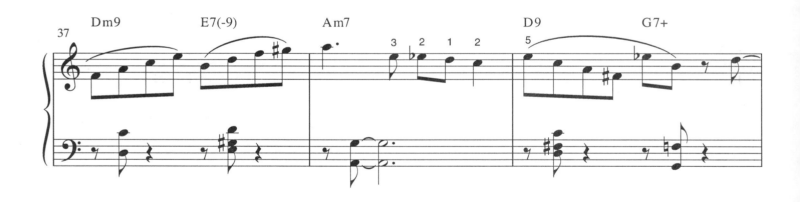

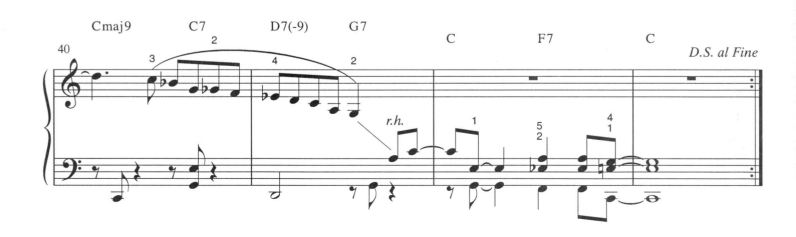

SHOAH

Andy LaVerne

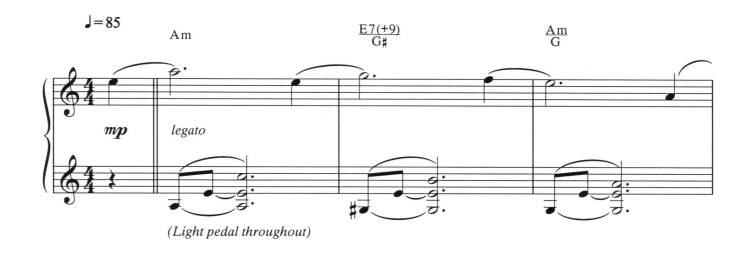

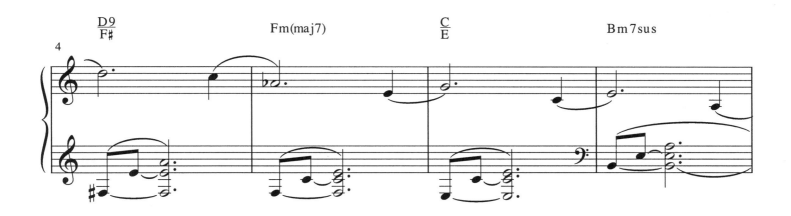

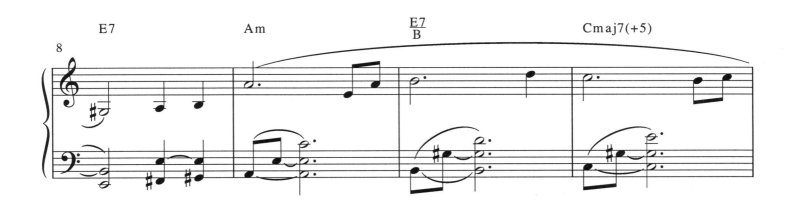

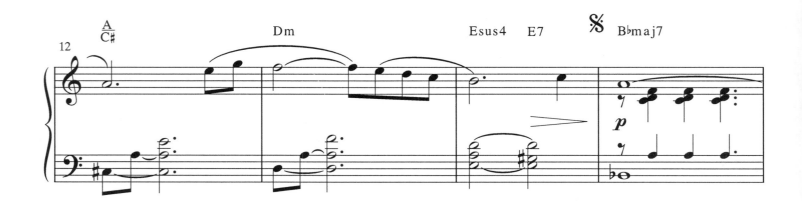

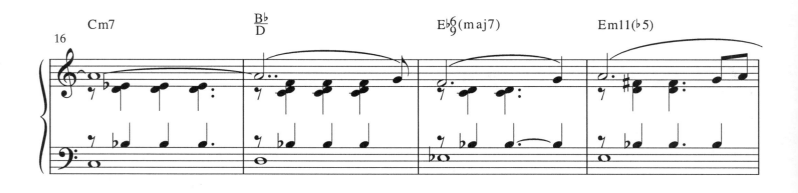

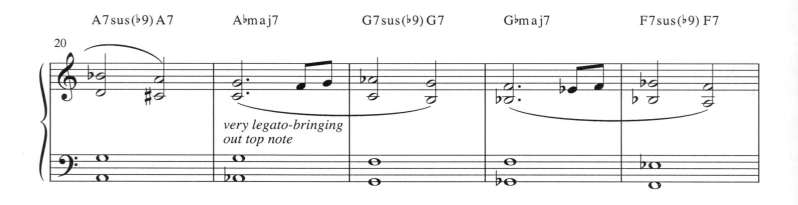

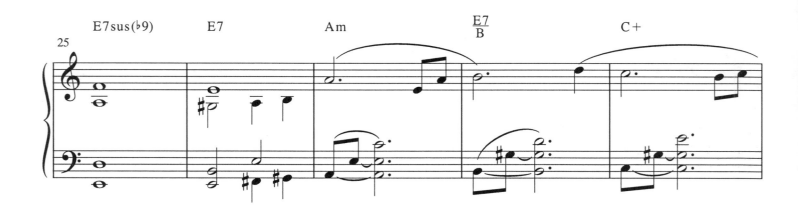

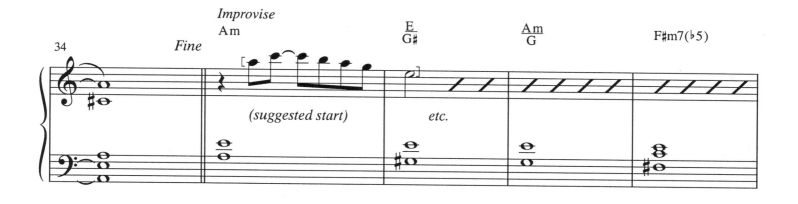

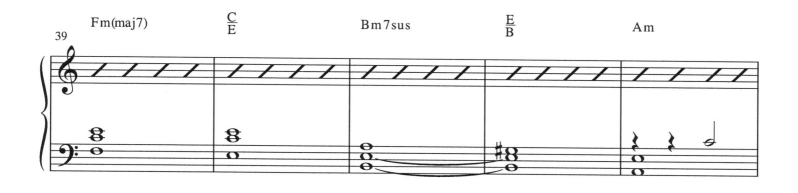

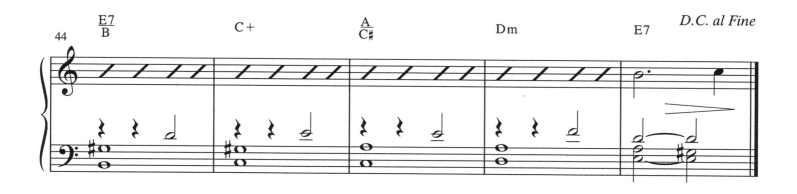

OLD FESS JOE RAG

Riccardo Scivales

Light and swingy (♩ = ca. 84)

Intro:

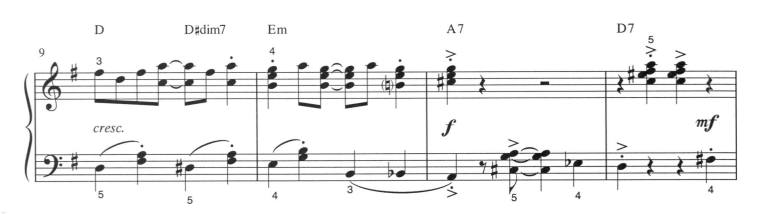

Note: in swing 8th note style (♫ = ♩♪)

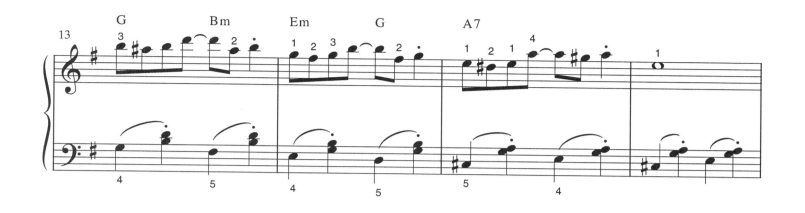

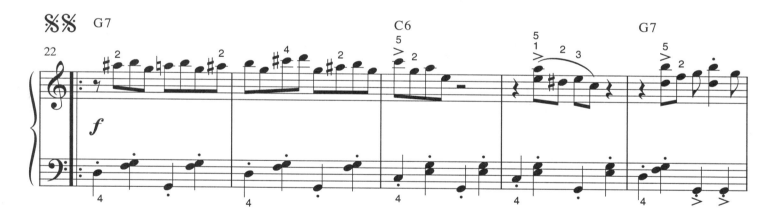

THE BROTHERS' BLUES

Riccardo Scivales

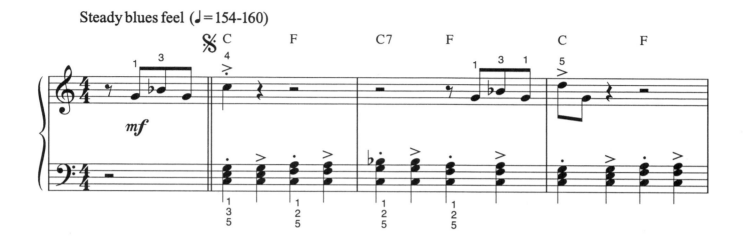

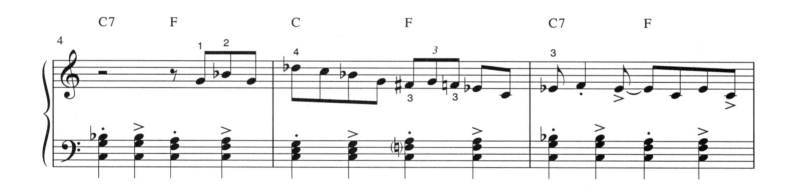

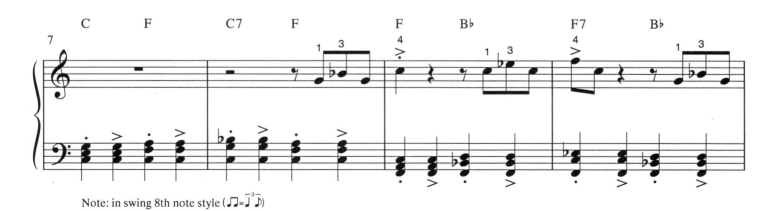

Note: in swing 8th note style (♫ = ♩⁼³♪)

RHYTHM AND BLUES

to Ed Shanaphy

Stuart Isacoff

With a swinging feel (♩ = 120)

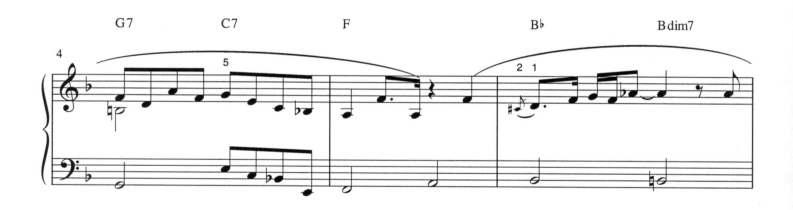

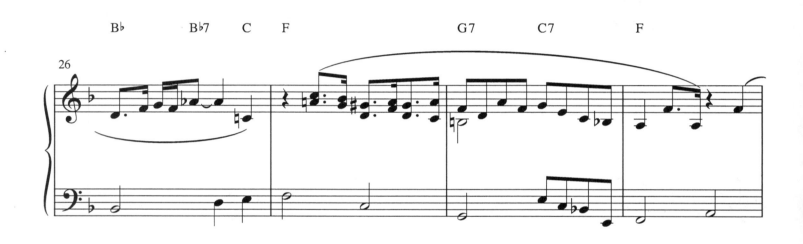

WIGGLE ROOM

Dick Hyman

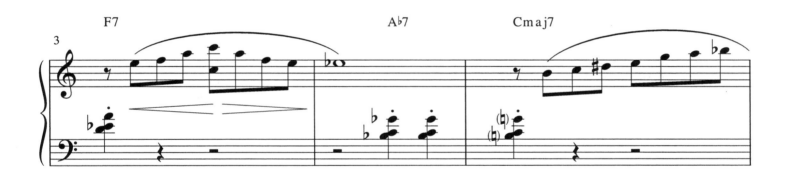

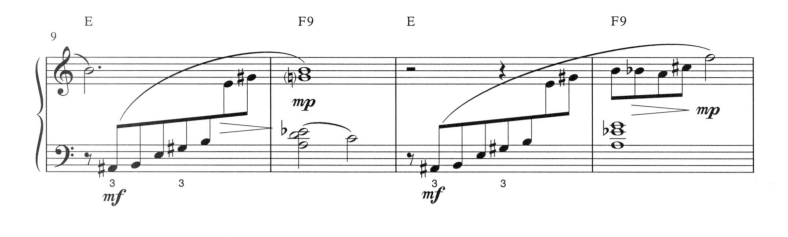

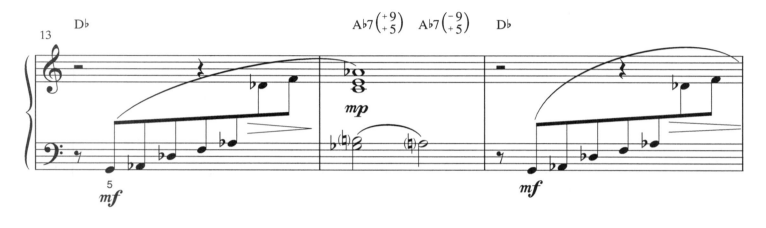

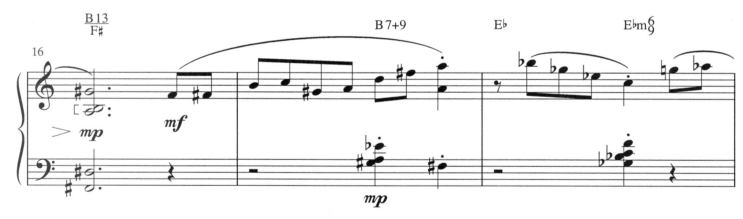

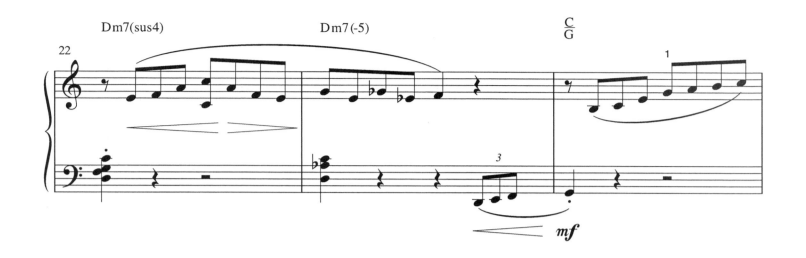

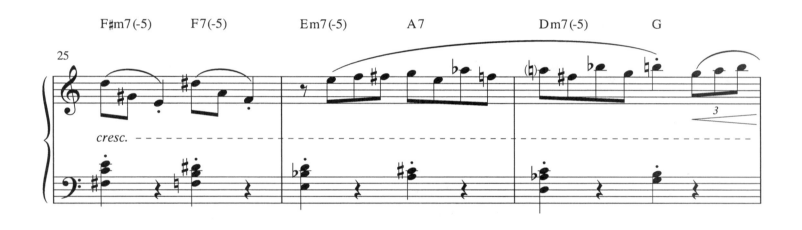

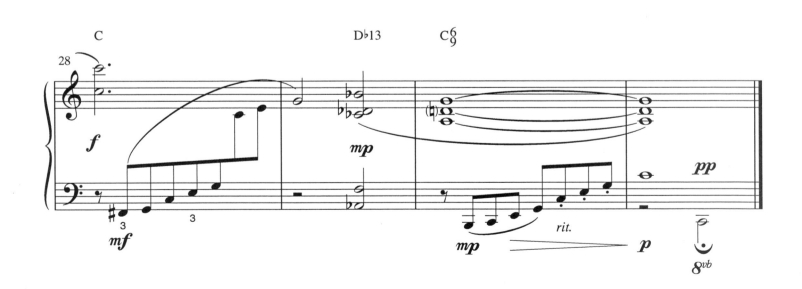

BOOGIE SPECIAL

Riccardo Scivales

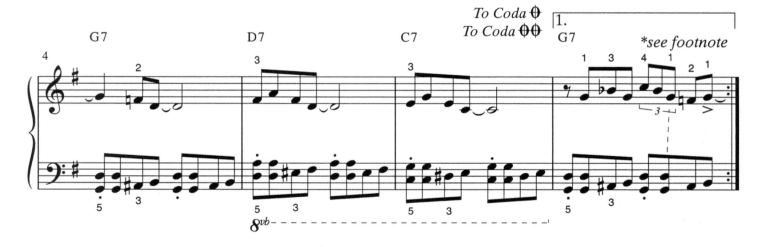

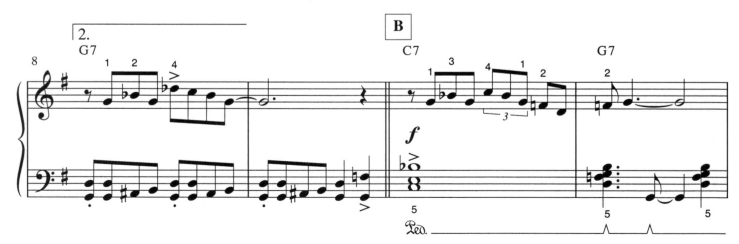

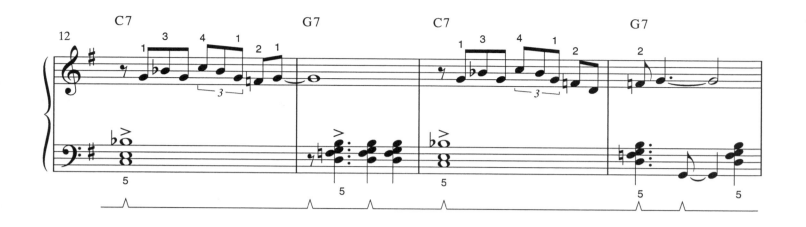

Repeat section B, then D.C. al Coda ⊕

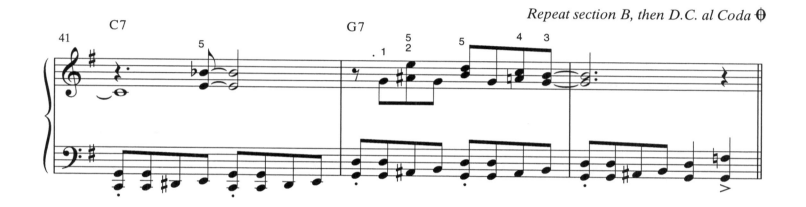

⊕⊕ *Coda*

Measure #7

*must actually
be played as:*

(swing 8ths)

YEARNING

Stuart Isacoff

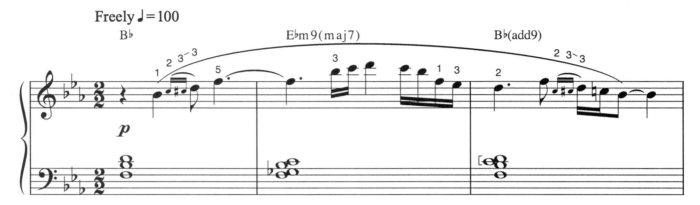

Change pedal with changes in harmony.

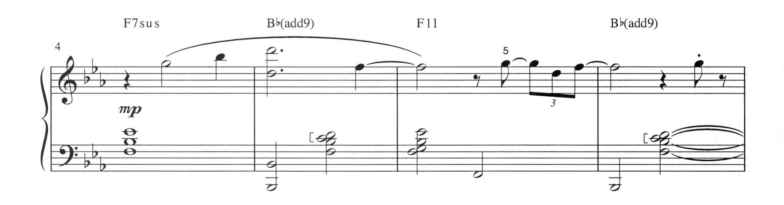

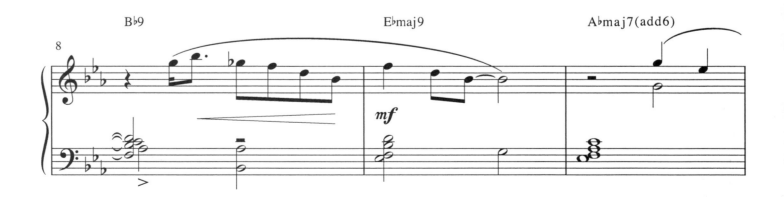

THE LOCKED STORE

Sarah Jane Cion

MEMORIES OF SCOTTY

to Scott LeFaro

Don Friedman

OLD AND NEW

Riccardo Scivales

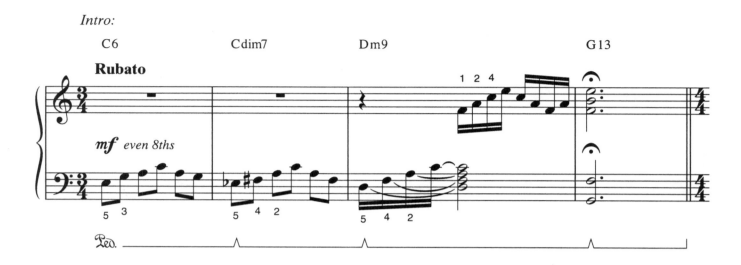

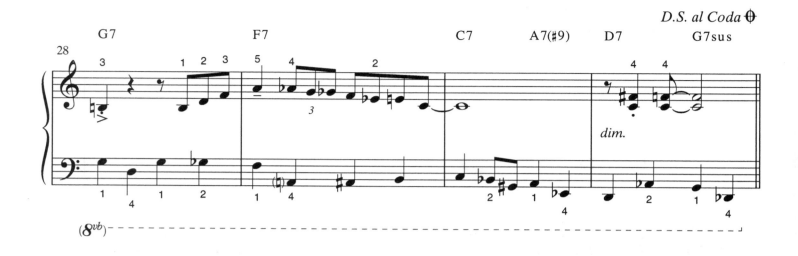

⊕ *Coda*

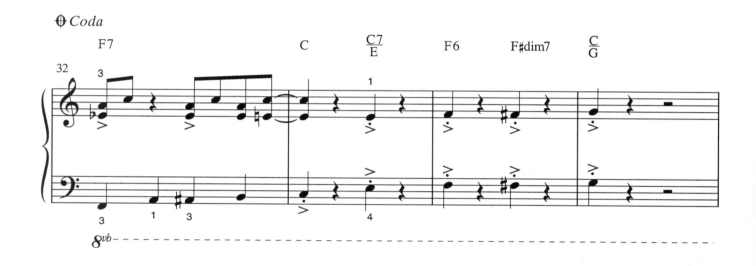

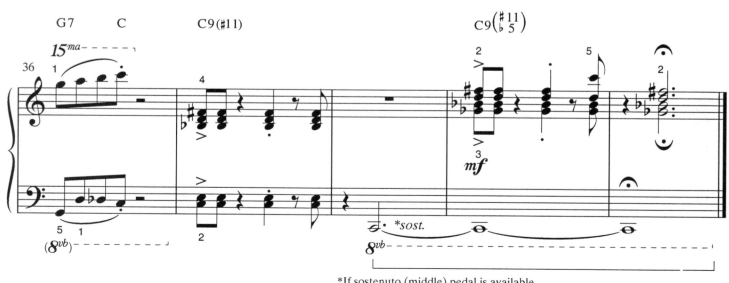

*If sostenuto (middle) pedal is available.

WHISTLIN' THE BLUES

Riccardo Scivales

Easy walking tempo (♩ = 116)

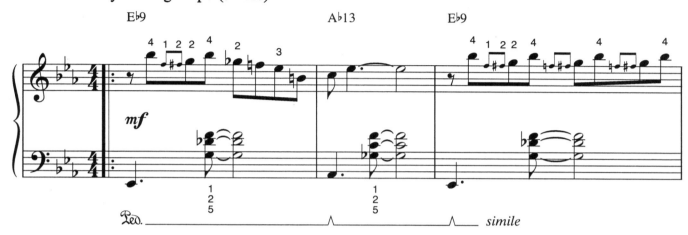

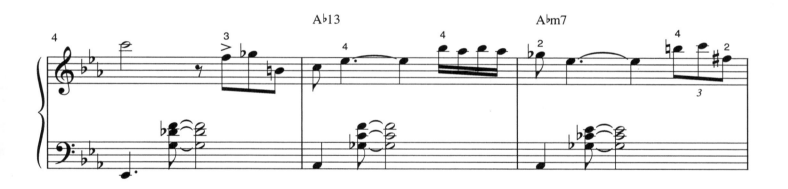

To Coda ⊕

Note: in swing 8th note style (♫ = ♩³♪)

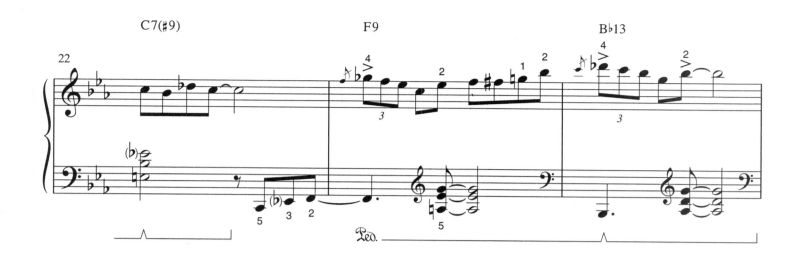

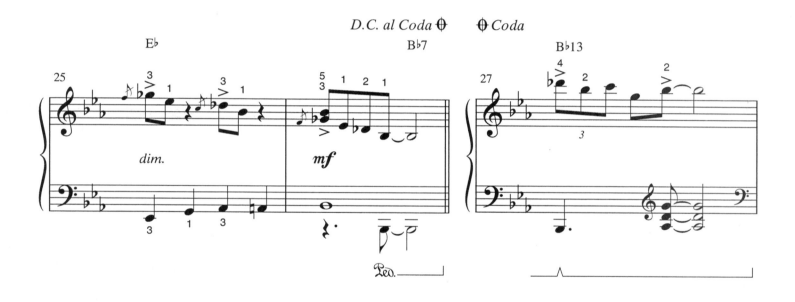

THE SAFFLOWER

Sarah Jane Cion

Jazz ballad

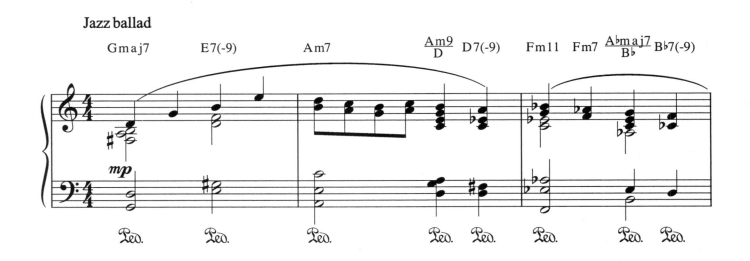

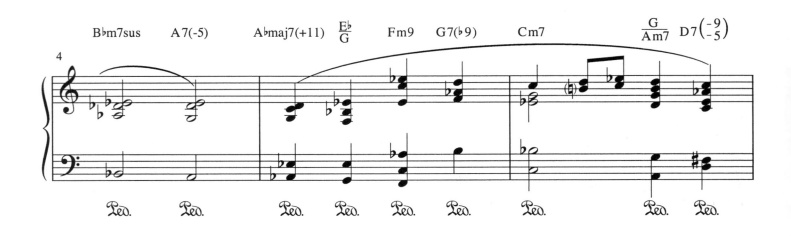

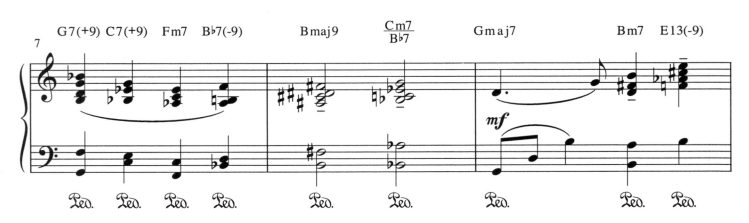

JAZZ ETUDE NO. 1

Noreen Lienhard

*Note: staccato mark under phrase denotes a detached light touch.

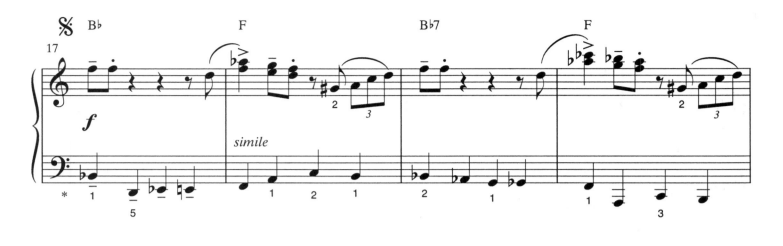

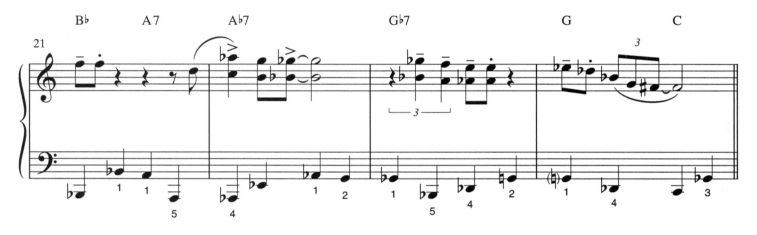

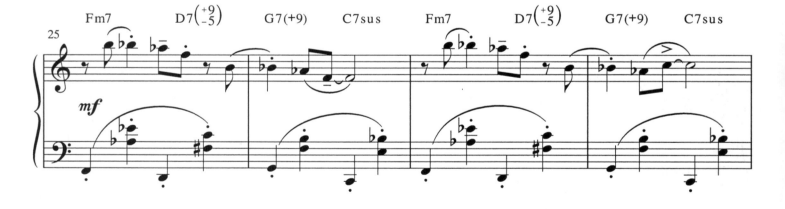

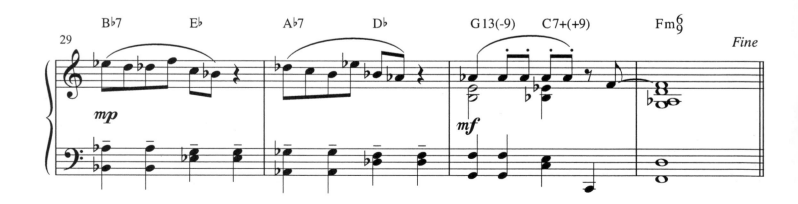

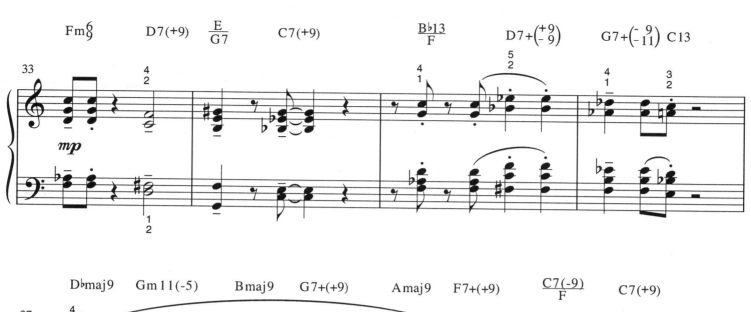

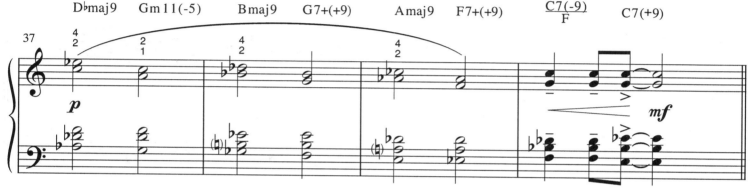

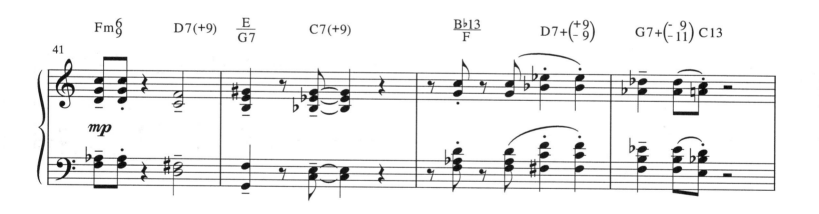

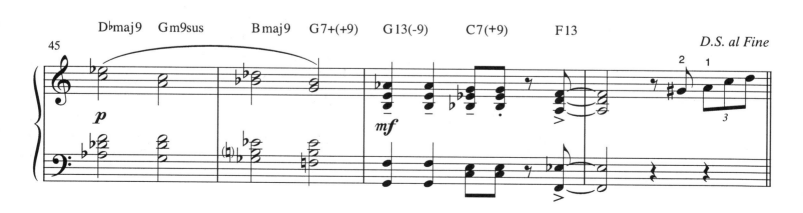

JAZZ ETUDE NO. 2

Noreen Lienhard

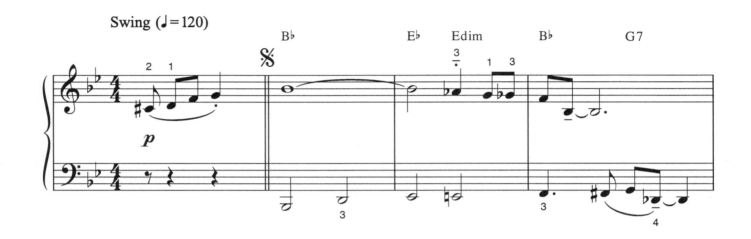

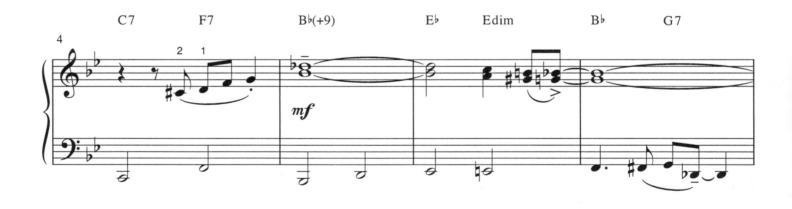

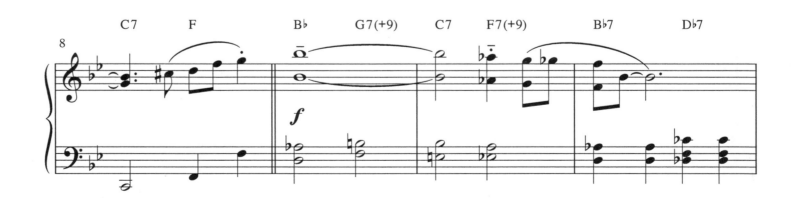

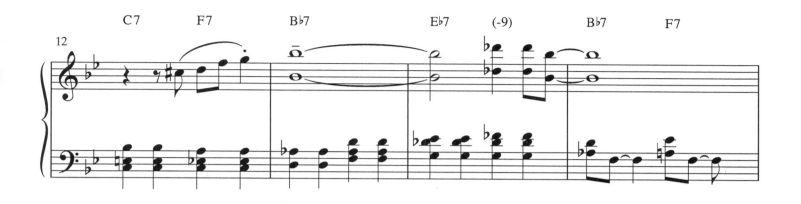

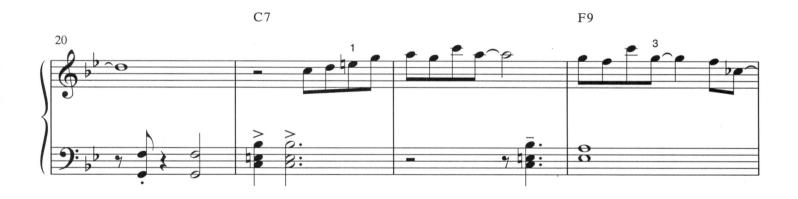

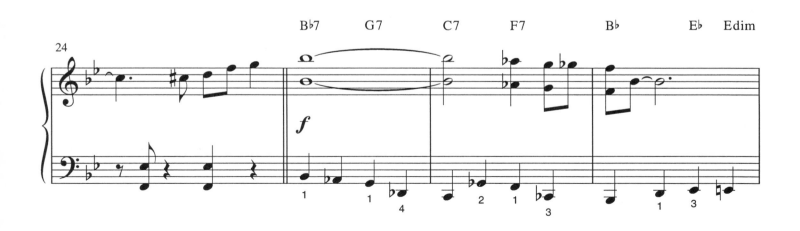

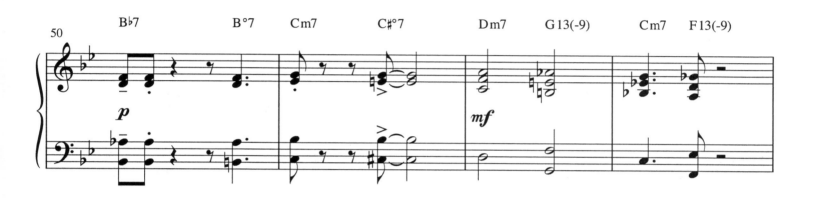

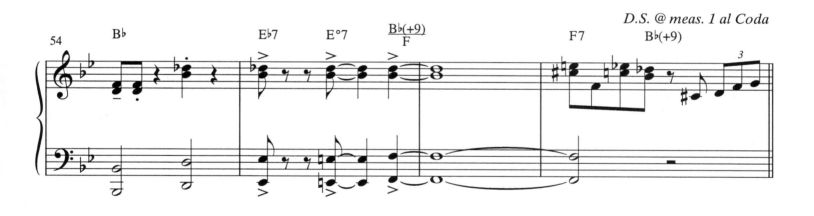

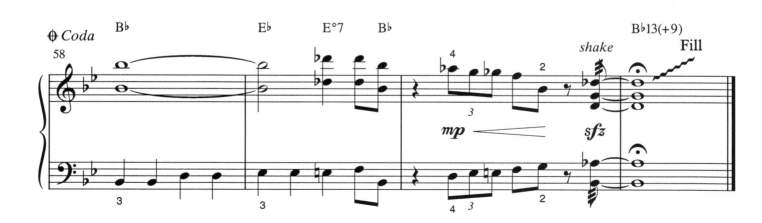

JAZZ ETUDE NO. 3

Noreen Lienhard

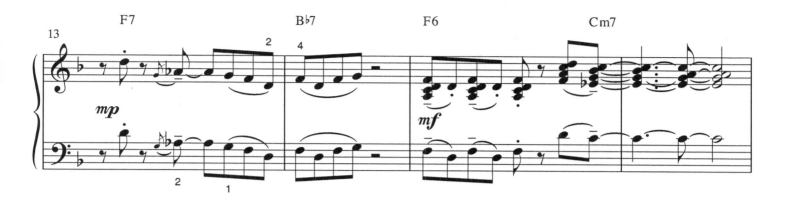

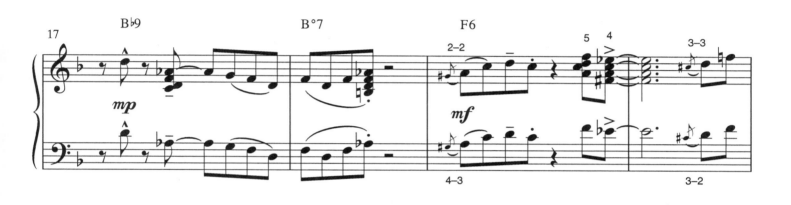

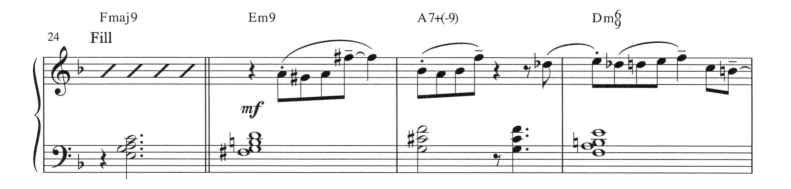

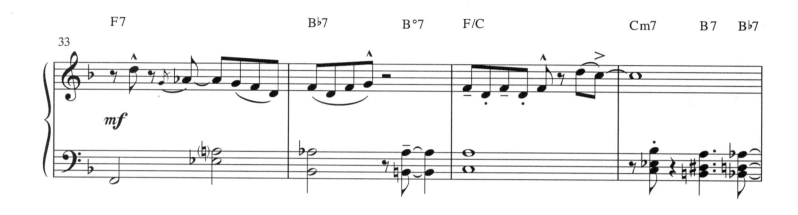

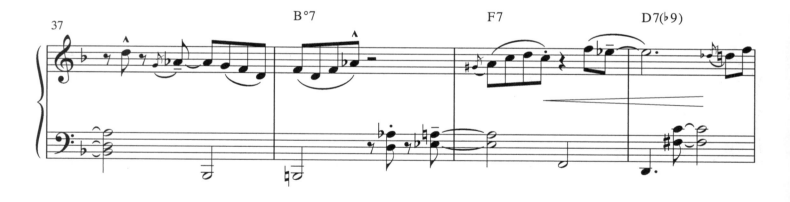

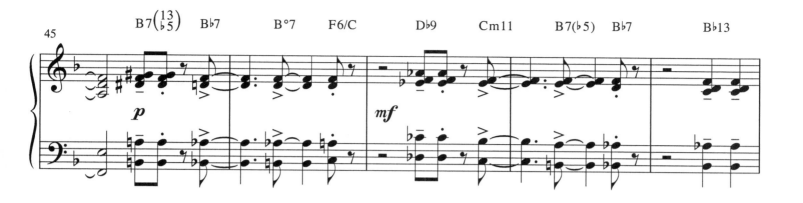

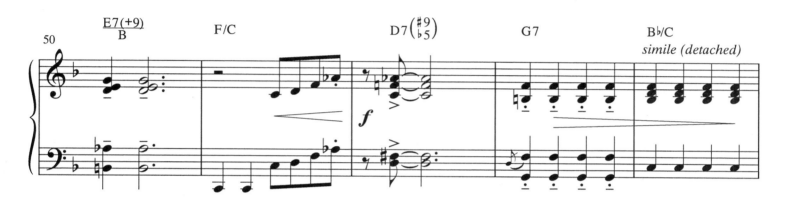

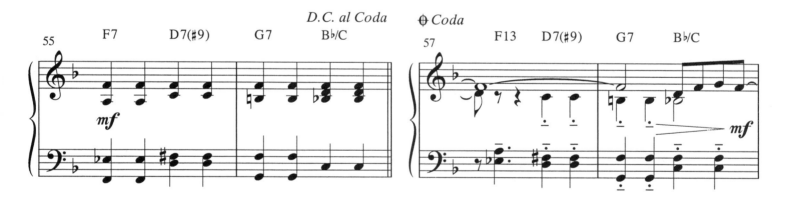

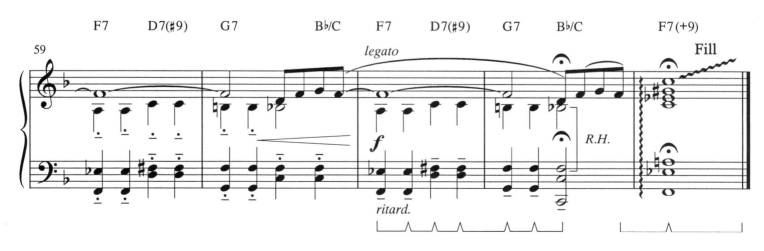

JAZZ ETUDE NO. 4

Noreen Lienhard

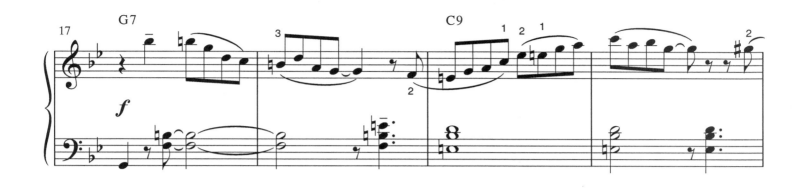

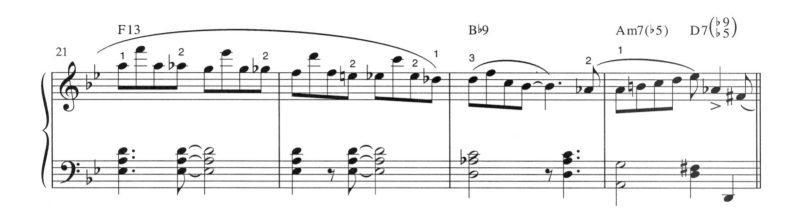

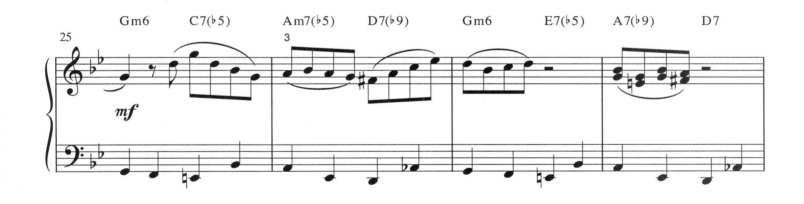

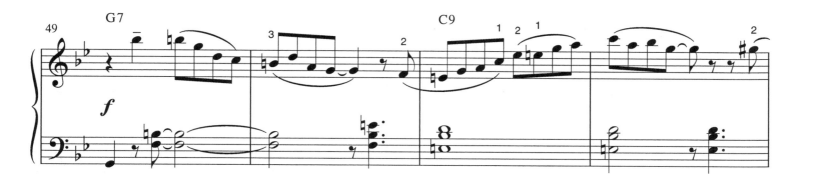

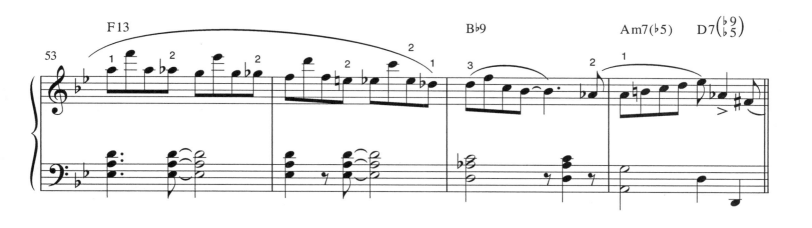

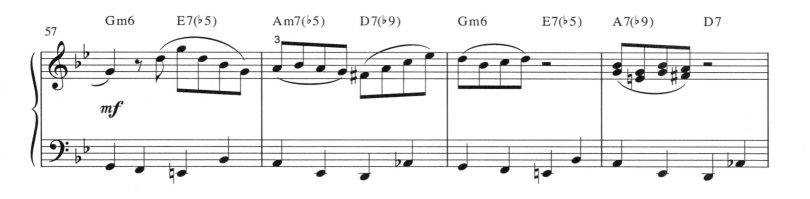

SPHERICAL

Joan Stiles

Medium swing

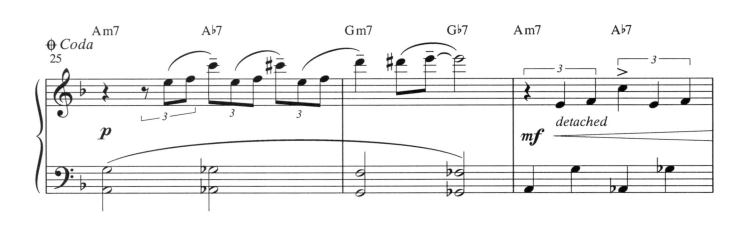

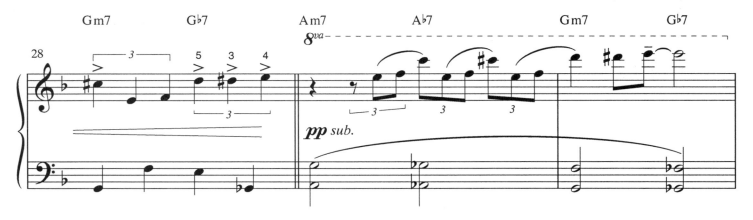

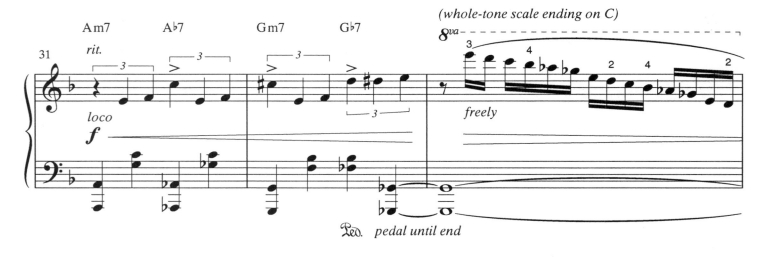

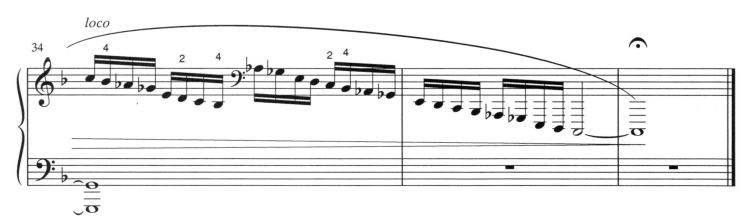

A RELATIVE MATCH

Sarah Jane Cion

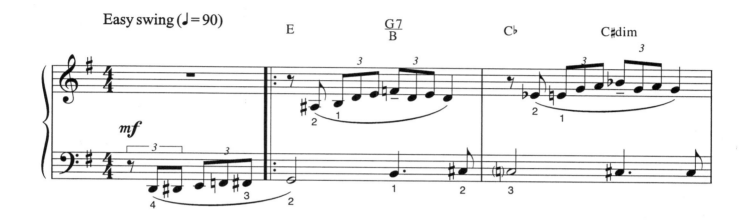

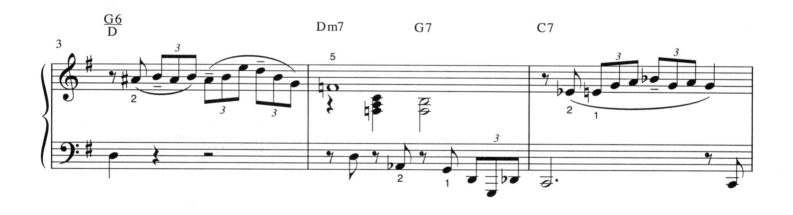

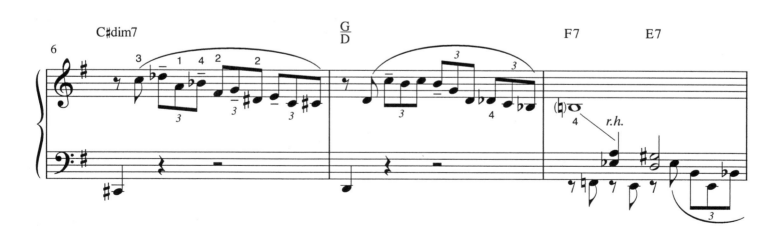

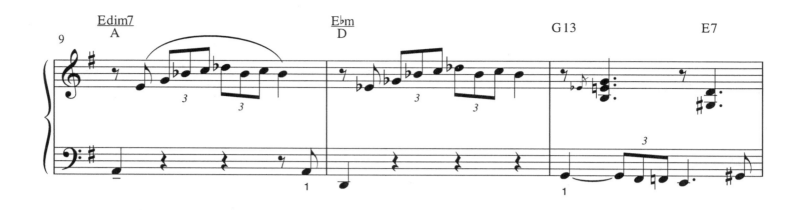

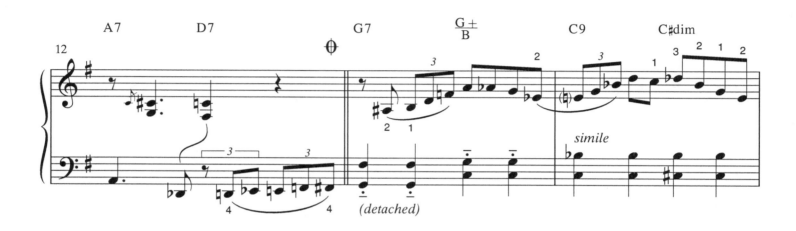

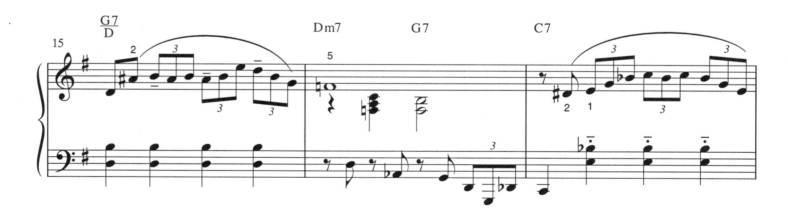

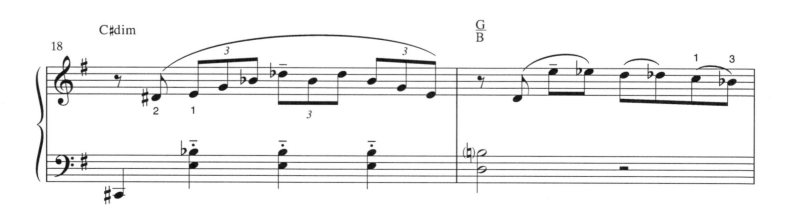

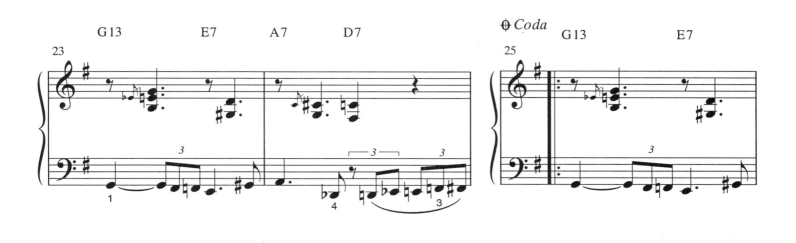

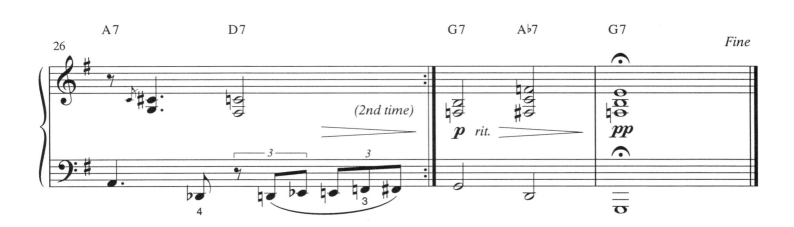

SUMMER'S END

Don Friedman

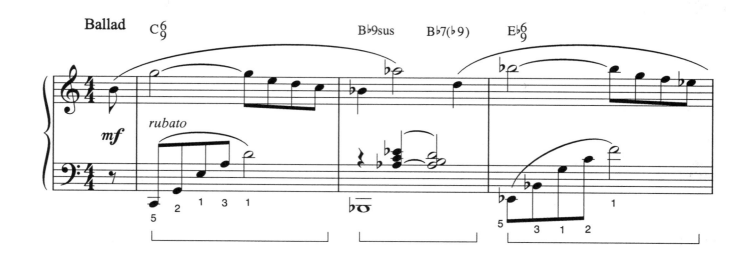

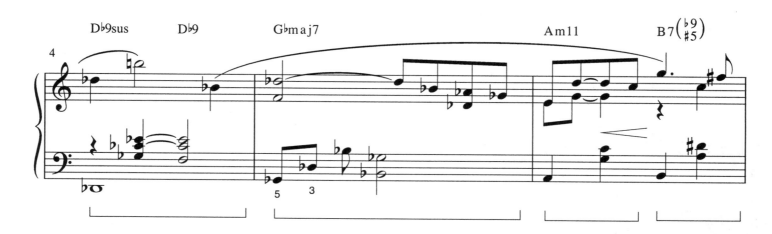

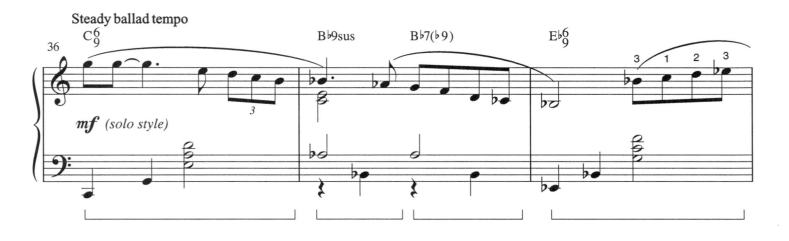

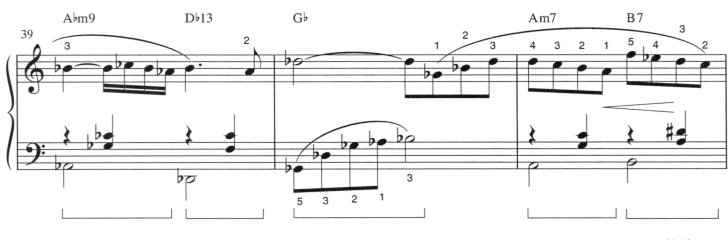

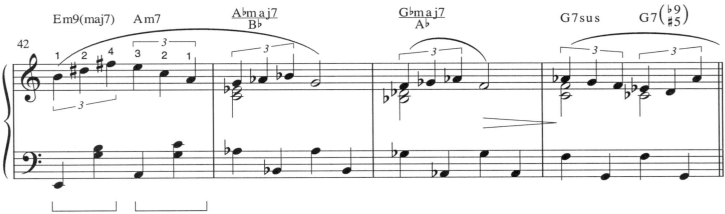

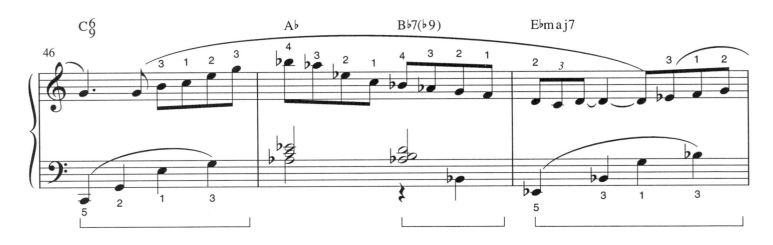

PARTY ON THE BEACH

Sarah Jane Cion

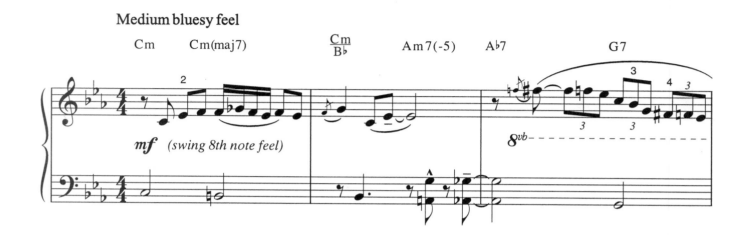

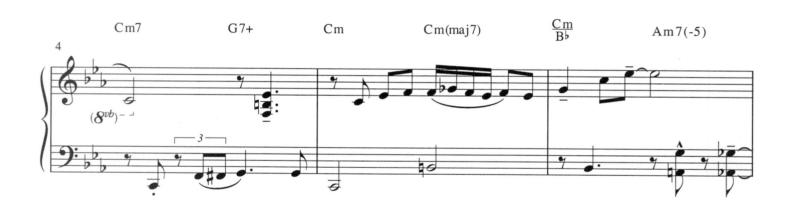

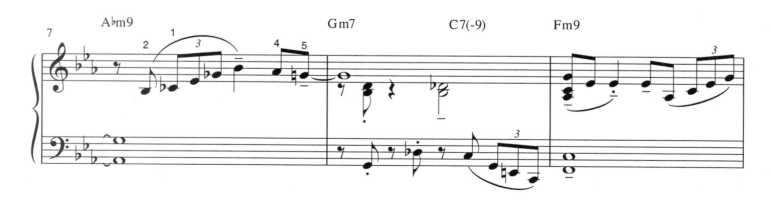

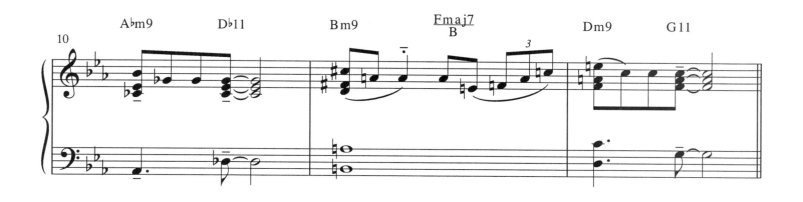

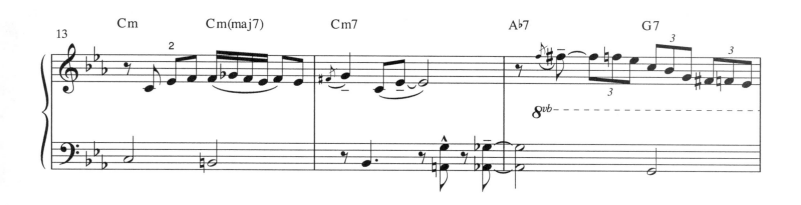

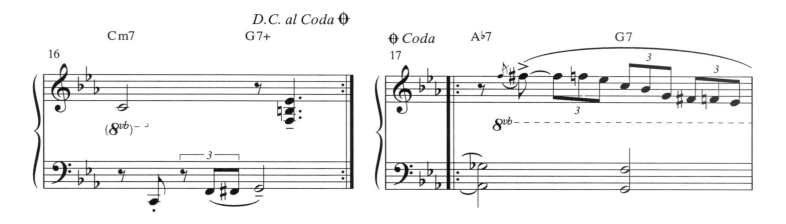

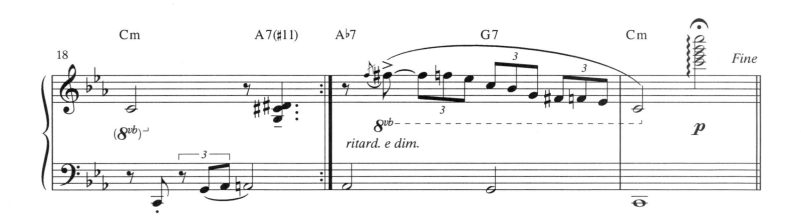

SHANIA

Andy LaVerne

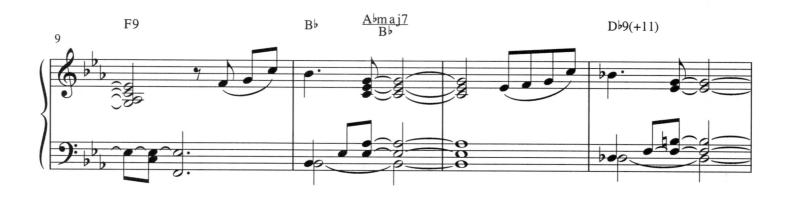

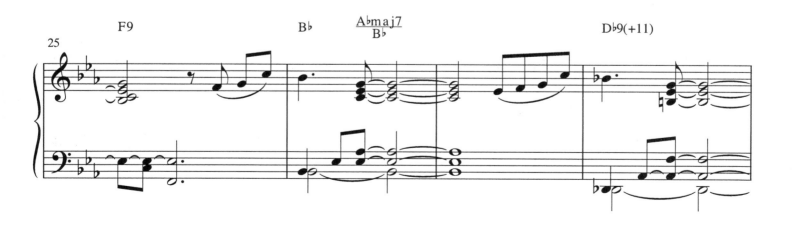

THREE SKETCHES

I. SUSAN'S SONG

Bill Dobbins

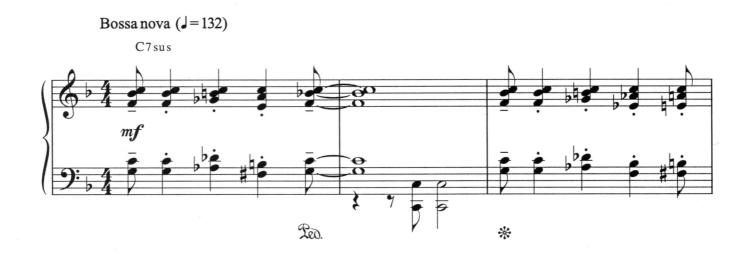

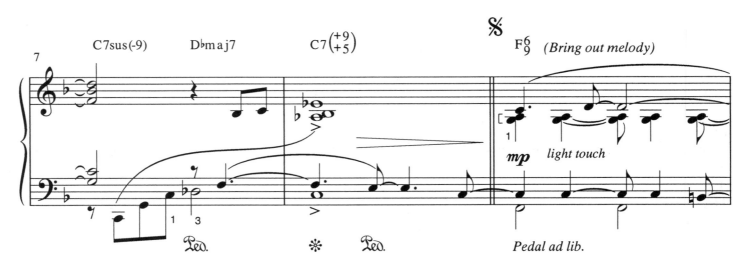

II. LULLABY FOR DAVID

Bill Dobbins

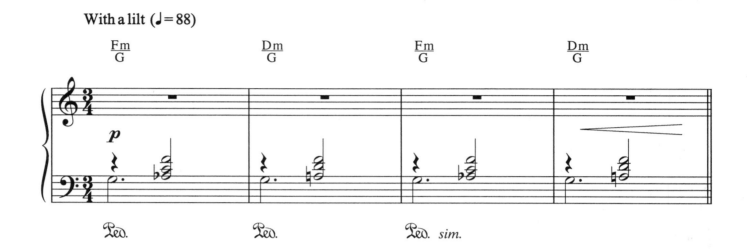

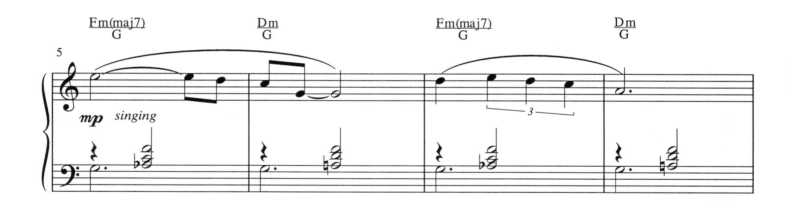

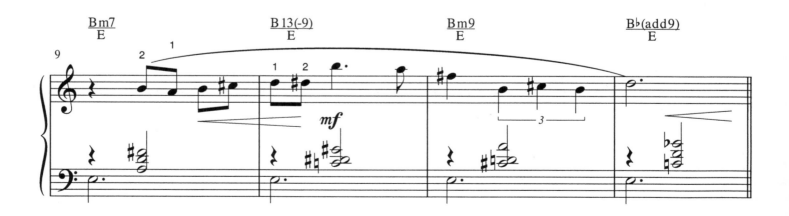

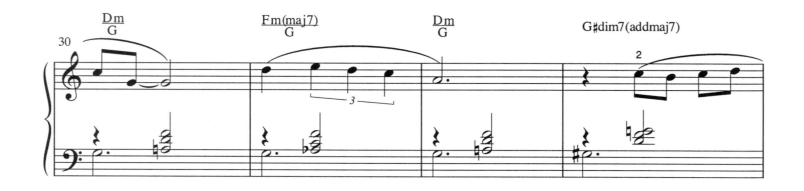

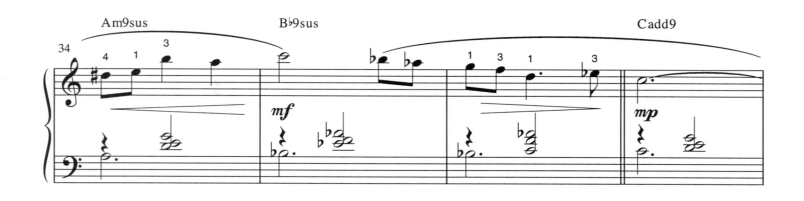

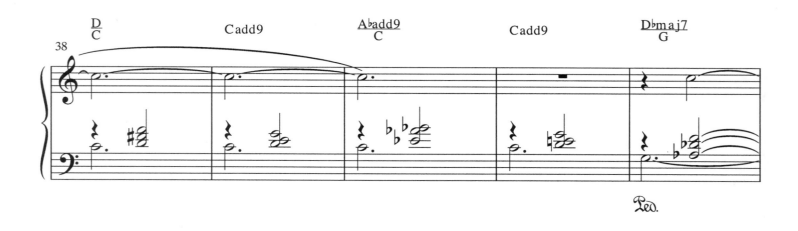

III. DANNY'S MOVES

Bill Dobbins

Medium shuffle (♩ = 144)

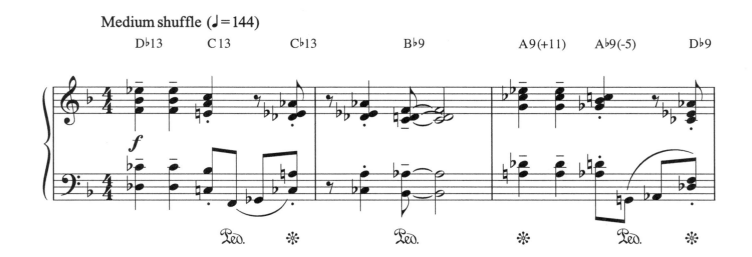

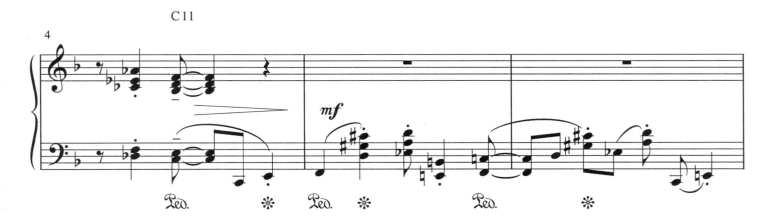

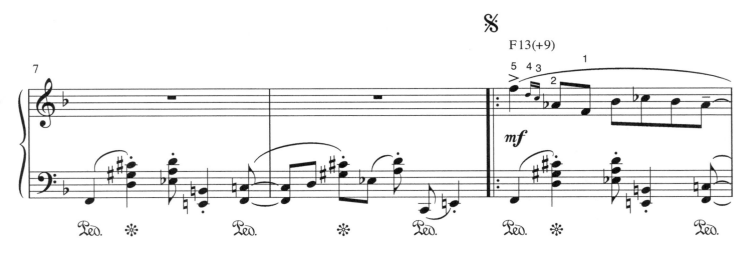

HOW 'BOUT IT?

Alan Simon

Medium swing (not too fast)*

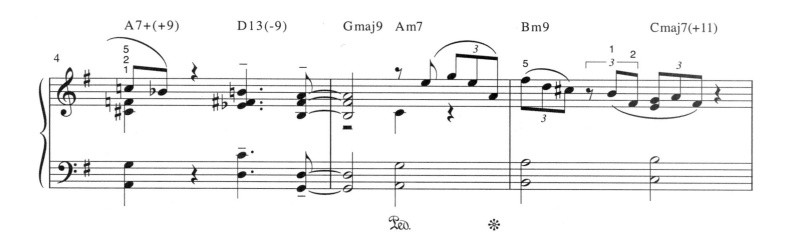

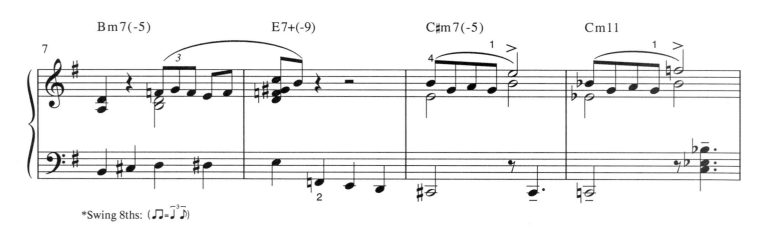

*Swing 8ths: (♫ = ♩ ♪)

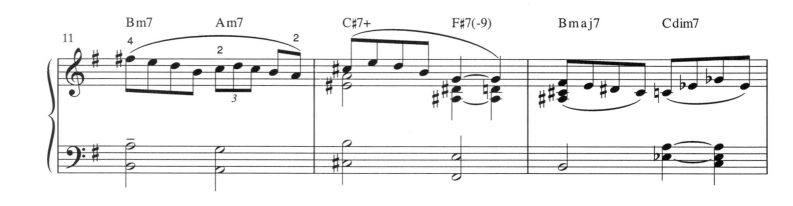

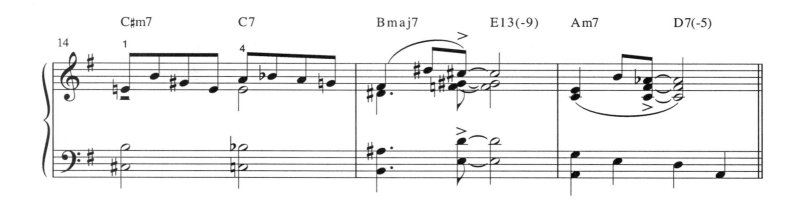

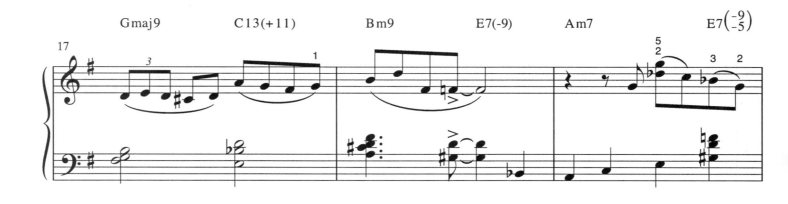

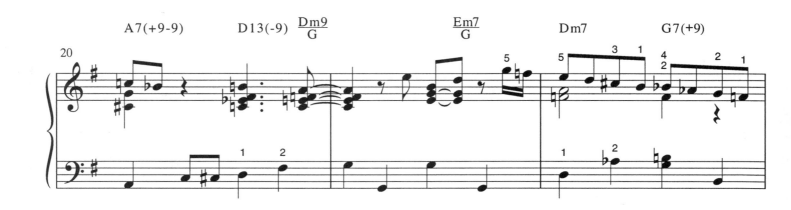

WISE SISTER

Dick Hyman

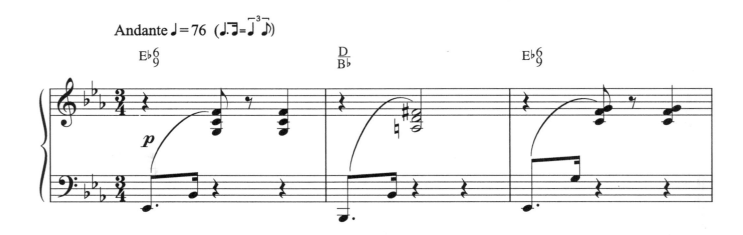

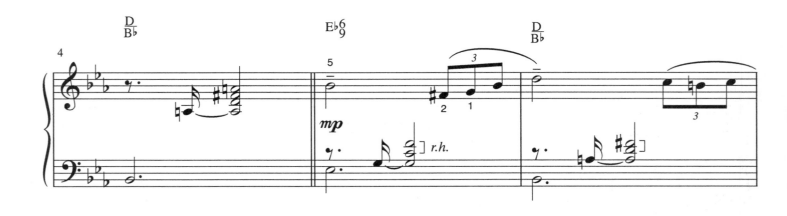

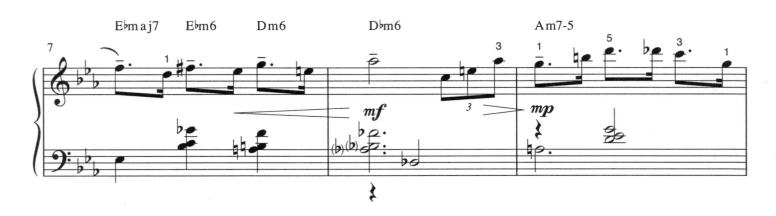

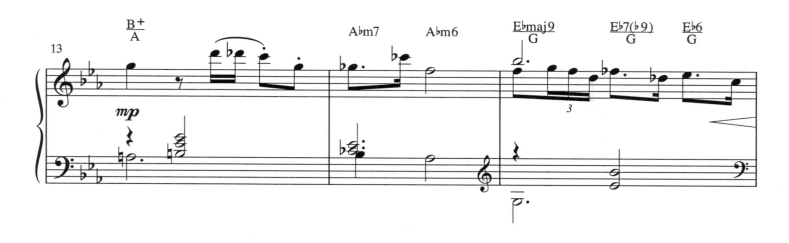

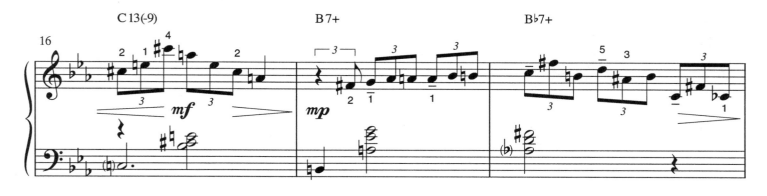

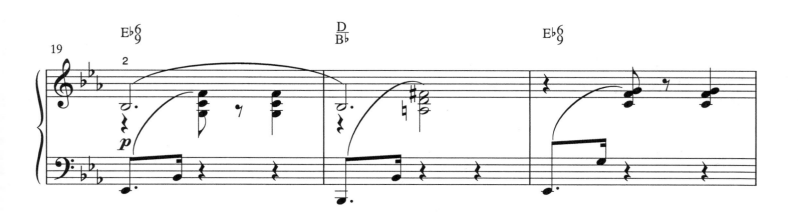

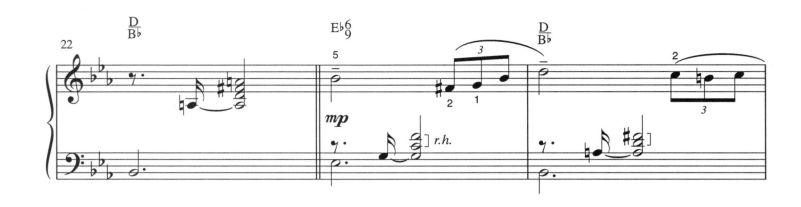

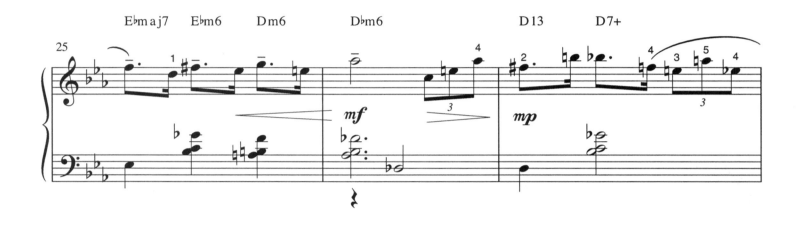

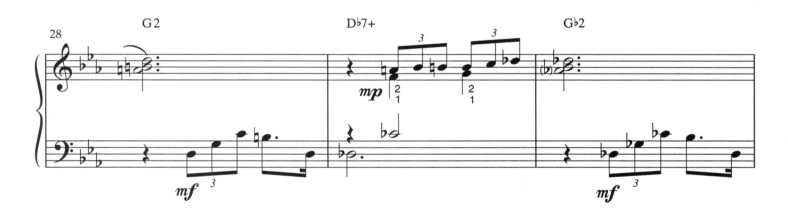

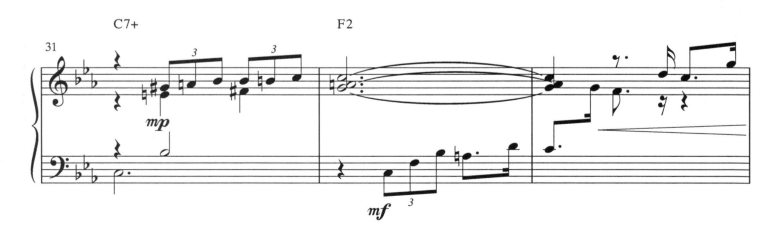

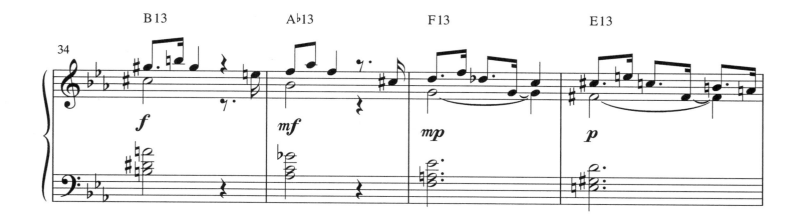

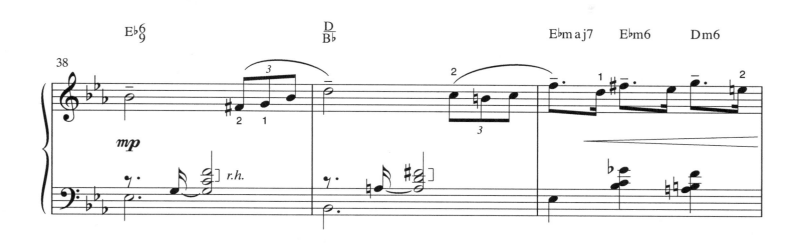

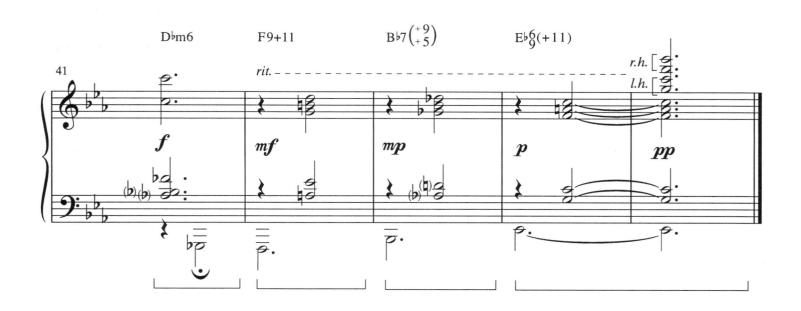

STRIDE PIANO PLAYIN' ON WAIKIKI

Dick Hyman

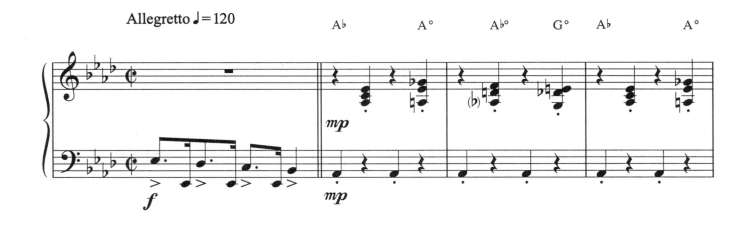

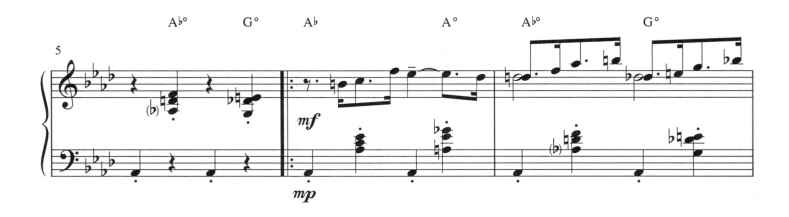

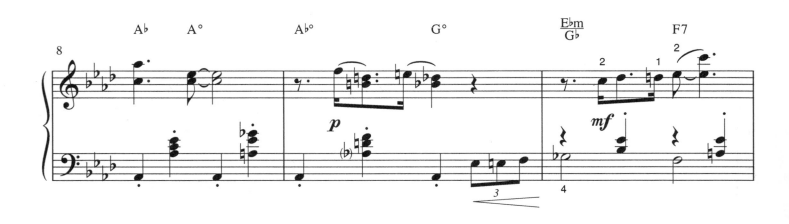